The CHEERLEADING Book

includes cheers, chants, and jumps!

STEPHANIE BREAUX FRENCH

CB

CONTEMPORARY
BOOKS

A TRIBUNE NEW MEDIA COMPANY

Library of Congress Cataloging-in-Publication Data

French, Stephanie Breaux, 1969–
    The cheerleading book / Stephanie Breaux French.
        p.   cm.
    ISBN 0-8092-3411-4 (paper)
    1. Cheerleading.   I. Title.
  LB3635.F74   1995
  791.640—dc20   94-47134
                                      CIP

To Ashley, Allison, and Danni,
future cheerleaders whom I love very much!

Cover and interior photos by Mark Battrell

Published by Contemporary Books, Inc.
Two Prudential Plaza, Chicago, Illinois 60601-6790
Manufactured in the United States of America
International Standard Book Number: 0-8092-3411-4
10   9   8   7   6   5   4   3   2   1

CONTENTS

PREFACE

In this book you will meet five wonderful cheerleaders, Kelly, Heidi, Rhoda, Kyomi, and Amanda. They started just where you are starting now—at the very, very, beginning. They have all been working on their cheerleading skills really hard and are happy to help you learn the important basics. If you like you can even write to them.

Just send the letters to:

International Cheerleading Association
10660 Barkley Road
Shawnee Mission, KS 66212

Good luck, and have a *blast!*

Rhoda

Kelly

Amanda

Kyomi

Heidi

ACKNOWLEDGMENTS

Thank you to Randy Neil and the International Cheerleading Association (ICA), for its vast knowledge in cheerleading and instruction. Randy, along with the ICA, has put out many incredibly useful instructional cheerleading books and videos. I hope this one will measure up!

Thanks to Pep Threads Uniforms, for the duds; to Mark French, Bill Lindsay, Randy and Darrin Bryant, and Lynwood Nixon, for your valuable input and patience.

And thanks also to Ashley and all of the cheerleaders of Blue Valley Northwest in Overland Park, Kansas, who posed for the cover; and to Kyomi and the cheerleaders of Trailridge Middle, for the inside photos.

Chapter 1 INTRODUCTION

Congratulations! You are now officially on your way to becoming a great cheerleader.

But first, you may want to learn a little about the history of this all-American activity. For instance, did you know that the first cheerleader was a boy? That's right, Johnny Cambell was his name, and he started a cheering sensation at the University of Minnesota in 1898. How did he do it? Well, basically, he was sitting in the stands with his schoolmates, and things were not going very well for Minnesota. In fact, they were losing. Johnny thought that maybe he could help his team out by showing some support, so he jumped out of the stands, faced the crowd, and started to yell: "Rah, Rah, Rah! Ski-U-Mah, Hoo-Rah! Hoo-Rah! Varsity! Varsity! MINN-E-SO-TAH!" Slowly the crowd began to catch on and yell with Johnny. Little by little the cheer grew louder and louder until suddenly the entire stadium was roaring with school spirit. Then the tide turned. Thanks to Johnny's leadership and the fans' support,

Minnesota went on to win that game and many more that season.

That great incident started the world cheering (or at least the United States) at sporting events. Cheerleaders were everywhere, leading the fans and encouraging their teams to victory after victory, until sometimes, the big win actually depended on whose crowd cheered the loudest. One amazing fact about Johnny Cambell's cheerleading debut is that, from the tiny spark that Johnny started, a fire blazed in its path which has yet to falter. In the 1920s, girls decided to get in on the action and the rest is history. Today cheerleading is more popular than ever! Through pep rallies, homecomings, and fund raisers, fans and faculty are behind their schools more than ever before. Cheerleaders have become one of the most important parts of American school spirit!

Cheerleading, however, is much much more than getting the crowds to yell cheers. As cheerleading has grown over the years, it has taken on another even more important role in America. Just think about it, whenever you attend a sporting event with your family or friends, what are your eyes glued to? The cheerleaders, of course! Every cheer, every sideline, every motion, everything they do just fascinates you, right? Of course! You would not have this book if that wasn't true. In fact, for every cheerleader who is out on a field in high school or even college, there are at least twelve more in the stands like you, watching closely, waiting for their chance to be in their own school colors yelling for their team to win. It has always been that way, which is why cheerleading is even more important than just yelling cheers. Cheerleaders have become role models. Not only do they excel in enthusiasm, but cheerleaders also have higher grades than many other high school groups. That's really cool; it shows how important it is to do your best in everything.

In this book are the basic tools you will need to be a total success in cheerleading. These include: Warming up your body by stretching; learning the hand, arm, and leg motions of cheering; knowing by heart the words to cheerleading chants and cheers; and finally, mastering one of the most exciting parts of cheerleading—jumps. Of course, there will be an opportunity to use your pom-poms, which give added color and excitement to many cheerleading routines.

If you learn all this, and practice, it is only a matter of time before you will take your place on the sidelines, to cheer for your team, your school, and your own stadium full of fans!

Chapter 2 WARM-UPS

Ever since the very first cheerleader belted out the very first cheer, cheerleading has been in a constant state of change. Perhaps that is one reason why it has continued to grow in popularity.

One thing's for sure: today's cheerleaders are not wimps!

If you are going to be a super cheerleader, you've got to make sure that you get in shape. All of the movements and jumps that you see cheerleaders doing are not as easy as they look. You really have to be fit to jump and cheer, have a ton of energy, and keep the crowd excited for a whole game. It takes work and practice to make sure you are ready.

Before you start trying any of the new cheerleading moves in this book, always remember to warm up your body properly. When you warm up by stretching, you are waking up your muscles and telling them that they are about to work hard on some new skills. Stretching before you do any physical activity will help keep you safe from injury. Stretching also helps to make your body more flexible. If you stretch every day you will soon have no trouble with those splits that you have seen cheerleaders perform, and when you start jumping, that will be easier, too! Here are some stretches that you can do every day to keep you safe and help prepare you for your adventures in cheerleading!

Neck Stretches

Side-to-Side Turn

Bring head
back toward
the front.

And then turn
head to the
right. Turn to
each side 10
times. This
means you will
be counting to
20.

Back straight,
hands on hips,
slowly turn
head to the
left.

Neck Stretches

Up-and-Down Lift

Standing with your back straight and your hands on your hips, slowly lower your chin to your chest.

Bring your head back up, facing straight forward.

Now lean your head back so you are looking at the sky. Do these 10 times each, so you will be counting to 20.

Shoulder Stretches

Shoulder Lift

Standing with your feet apart, back straight, and head up, slowly lift your shoulders straight up as high as you can.

Lower your shoulders to a relaxed position. Repeat slowly 10 times, squeezing tightly as you reach the top.

Shoulder Stretches

Shoulder Roll—Backward

Roll them gently backward.

Standing with your feet apart, back straight, and head up, slowly lift your shoulders.

Bring them down and back around to the starting position. Do this 10 times.

Shoulder Stretches

Shoulder Roll—Forward

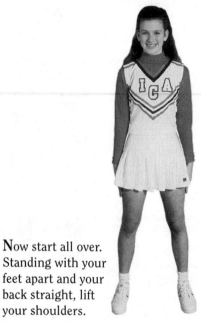

Now start all over.
Standing with your
feet apart and your
back straight, lift
your shoulders.

This time roll
them gently
forward.

Bring them
down and back
around to the
starting position.
Do this 10 times
also.

Shoulder Stretches

. . . .

Arm Across Body

Standing with your feet apart and back straight, bring your left arm straight across your body and use your right arm to pull it to your chest. Stretch for about 30 seconds.

Now do the same with your right arm. Again for about 30 counts. Make sure that the arm you are stretching is steady and you are not bouncing.

Shoulder Stretches

Arm Over Head

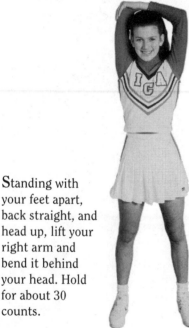

Standing with your feet apart, back straight, and head up, lift your right arm and bend it behind your head. Hold for about 30 counts.

Use your other hand to push down just a little on your elbow to help the stretch.

Now do the same with your left arm, again for 30 counts. Remember not to bounce.

Shoulder Stretches

Arm Circles—Forward

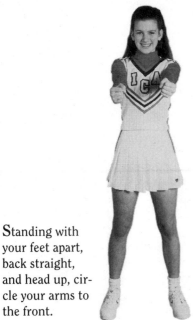

Up and
around
your head.

Standing with
your feet apart,
back straight,
and head up, cir-
cle your arms to
the front.

Back behind
you and
around to
the front
again. Do
these front
arm circles
10 times.

Shoulder Stretches

Arm Circles—Backward

Still standing with your feet apart, circle your arms backward.

Bring them down by your legs.

And circle them back up and around to the front again. Do the back arm circles 10 times, too!

Shoulder Stretches

Wrist Turn

Clasp your hands in front of your body as if there were a bee inside.

As if the bee were flying from side to side, and in all directions, bend your wrists sideways.

You can also have the bee circle around so your wrists circle too. Do these for about 20 counts.

Leg Stretches

Butterfly Stretch

Sit on the ground and bring your feet in front of you so that the soles of your feet are touching. Make sure your head is up and your shoulders are straight.

Pull your feet as close to your body as you can while still feeling comfortable and use your elbows to slowly push your knees to the floor. Hold this position without bouncing for 30 slow seconds.

Leg Stretches

Squat Stretch

Keeping your head and shoulders straight, stand with your feet double wide, with your feet and knees turned out.

Lower your body to a squat position, letting your hands slide toward your ankles. Hold for 30 slow seconds without bouncing.

Leg Stretches

Straddle Stretch

Standing with your legs double-shoulder-width apart, and your feet flat on the floor, slowly lower your body to your right knee as far as you can without any pain. Be careful not to bounce.

Now move your body to the center, as low as you can without bouncing.

Then, move your body to the left knee, keeping your body close to your knee. Again, no bouncing.

Leg Stretches

Straddle Stretch with Toes Flexed

Now flex your toes and repeat the stretch on the right side.

Again slowly move toward the middle.

Now with toes flexed, move to the left again. Hold each stretch for a count of 30 without bouncing.

Leg Stretches

Pike Stretch

Stand with your feet together; slowly roll down bringing your body toward your knees. Go as far as you can without straining your muscles or bouncing. Hold each stretch for 30 seconds.

Now cross your left leg over your right, and again go down as far as you can without straining.

Cross your right leg over your left and repeat the stretch.

Leg Stretches

Ankle Circles

Sitting on the ground, cross your right leg over your left.

Use your hands to slowly circle your foot around. Circle 20 times.

Leg Stretches

Ankle Circles

Now cross your left leg over your right.

Circle the other foot slowly 20 times as well.

Chapter 3 MOTIONS

As mentioned earlier, if you want to become a great cheerleader, you must begin with the basics. The "cheering" part of cheerleading is one of the basics and is simple once you learn how. Cheers are made up of hand, arm, and leg motions. The secret to looking really super while cheering is doing the motions sharply and placing them just right.

A chant or sideline is very much like a cheer except it is shorter. You repeat it three or four times so your fans can catch on easily and help you yell for your team. Though cheers and chants both have the same kinds of motions, chants can be quicker. Some chants are not meant to be sharp but bouncy, and some chants only have one motion—clapping!

Let's get started learning those motions, shall we? Once you get used to the feel of the motions, you should practice them in front of a full-length mirror to make sure you are doing them just right. Later on, you might want to get a friend or group of friends to work with you; you can take turns helping each other with your sharpness.

Hand Motions

Fists

This is the pinkie side of your fist because your pinkie is facing to the crowd.

This is the thumb side of your fist because now your thumb is facing to the crowd.

Buckets

These are called buckets because it looks like you may be holding buckets by their handles.

Candlesticks

Turn your fists so that your fingers are facing forward, as if you are holding candlesticks out to your sides.

Hand Motions

Blades

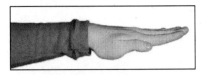

To make blades, open your hands flat and push all your fingers as close together as you can. Make sure that you don't forget to tuck in your thumb.

Blades are hard to perfect but are really neat when you do them right.

Arm Motions

Daggers

Make sure that your fists are right at your shoulders and your elbows are tucked into your sides.

Touchdown

Your arms should be straight over your head and right by your ears with your fists turned so that the pinkie holes are showing.

High V

Bring your arms up so that they make a V. Your elbows should be straight with your fists turned so that the thumb holes show.

Arm Motions

Broken High V

Bend your arms in to create a broken high V with your pinkies to the front.

T Motion

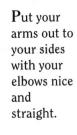

Put your arms out to your sides with your elbows nice and straight.

Broken T

Bend your arms in and make a broken T.

Arm Motions

Low V

Broken Low V

Low Touchdown

Bring your arms down so your V is upside down. Remember, keep your arms straight.

Bend your arms in and now you have a broken low V.

Put your arms straight down, right on the side of your legs.

Arm Motions

Hands on Hips

This is an easy one. Just remember to keep your hands in a tight fist.

Right Diagonal

You are going to make a straight line across your body with your right arm up and your left arm down. These are kind of hard to get perfect.

Broken Right Diagonal

Just bend your arms toward your chest, keeping your elbows in a diagonal line.

Arm Motions

Left Diagonal

Now make a straight line across your body with your left arm up and your right arm down.

Broken Left Diagonal

Bend your arms in to make a broken left diagonal.

Punch Straight Out

While making fists and keeping your hands nice and straight, lift your arms out in front of your body so it looks like you are punching.

Arm Motions

Punch Up—Right

While making a fist, lift your right arm so that it is straight up over your head, right next to your ear. Keep your other fist on your hip.

Punch Up—Left

While making a fist, lift your left arm so that it is straight up over your head, right next to your ear. Keep your other fist on your hip.

Right L

Your right arm is straight by your ear and your left is out to the side. This even looks like an L.

Arm Motions

Left L

This time your left arm is straight up by your ear and your right arm is out to your side. This makes a backward L.

Right Front Across

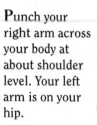

Punch your right arm across your body at about shoulder level. Your left arm is on your hip.

Left Front Across

Your left arm is punched out across the front of your body, and your right arm is on your hip.

Arm Motions

Left Punch Out and Right Dagger

Your left arm is in a front punch, and your right arm is in a dagger.

Right High V and Left Broken Low V

Your right arm is in a high V, and your left arm is in a broken low V.

Left Broken T and Right T

Your left arm is in a broken T, and your right arm is in a T.

Once you learn the basic motions, you can combine any of them to create a totally new motion. These are just a few of the thousands of combinations you can create.

Leg Motions

Right Lunge

This is how your bent leg should look during a lunge.

Left Lunge

Front Lunge

Stand with your back straight, shoulders and hips forward, and head up. Now move your left leg so that it is as straight as possible. Bend your right leg so that your knee is directly over your ankle.

Standing with the same good posture, this time move your right leg straight out so your left leg is bent.

Now put one leg out behind you very straight so that your front leg is in a bent lunge position.

34

Leg Motions

Right Liberty Hitch

Left Liberty Hitch

Right Side Liberty Hitch

Stand straight, with shoulders and head up. Now just lift your right leg so that the inside of your foot is even with your left knee. Don't forget to point your toe and keep your hands on hips.

Same as the right, just switch legs.

This is the same as the liberty hitch, except you turn your body to one side.

Leg Motions

. . . .

Left Side Liberty Hitch

Left Hip Dip

Right Hip Dip

Same as the right, but with the left leg up.

Bend your knees just a little and tilt your weight to the left side. Make sure you keep your back straight and head up.

Bend your knees just a little and tilt your weight to the right side. Keep your body straight, with shoulders and head up.

. . .

Chapter 4 CHANTS

Let's put together some of the motions you have just learned, add some words, and learn some real cheerleading chants!

You should read all the words in the chant first before you begin to use body movements. This will help you to concentrate on the beat.

Every pause or clap (even with your poms) that you see creates a different beat, making all your chants different and fun. Say them out loud a couple of times so you know them without looking. Then it will be easy to put the motions with the words.

Don't forget to smile!

STEAL IT *(clap clap)* STEAL IT *(clap clap)*

Steal
Right arm in T.
Left arm in
broken T.

It
Right arm in
broken T. Left
arm in T.

(pause)
Stand
straight,
feet apart.
Clap.

(pause)
Clap.

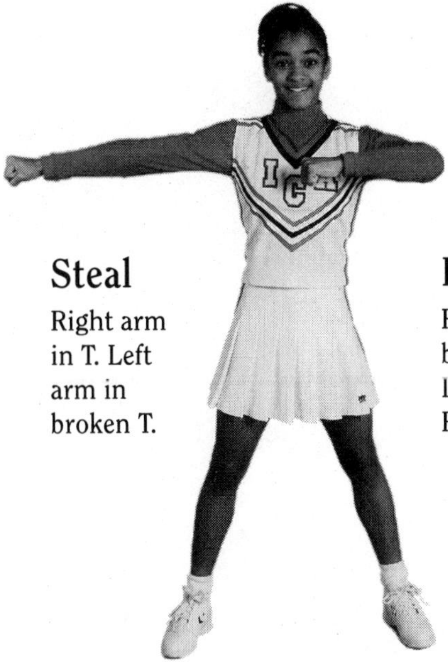

Steal
Right arm
in T. Left
arm in
broken T.

It
Right arm in
broken T.
Left arm in T.
Repeat claps.

TOUCHDOWN, TOUCHDOWN, SIX POINTS MORE *(pause)*

Touch
Touchdown
motion.

Down
Daggers motion.

Touch
Touchdown
motion.

Down

Daggers motion.

Six

Place your right arm over your left arm flat in front of your chest.

Points

Broken T motion.

More
T motion.

(pause)
Arms at your
sides. Repeat.

ONE, TWO, THREE, FOUR, EAGLE TEAM, RAISE THAT SCORE

One

Here you can use your pom-poms. Right arm on hip. Left arm in low V.

Two

Low V.

Three

Left diagonal.

Four
High V.

Eagle
Clap.

Team
Clap.

Raise That

Right arm in dagger. Left arm on hip.

Score

Right arm punch up. Left arm on hip. Repeat.

EAGLES *(clap)* ATTACK *(clap)* PUSH 'EM WAY BACK

Eagles
Right lunge.
Right arm on
hip. Left arm
across body.

(pause)
Stand straight,
feet apart. Clap.

Attack
Left lunge. Right
arm across body.
Left arm on hip.

46

(pause)

Stand straight,
feet apart. Clap.

Push 'Em

Hop. Feet
together, little
bend in the
knees. Daggers.

Way

Lean forward,
bend at waist,
legs straight.
Arms both punch
out.

Back

Stand feet together. Hands on hips.

Eagles

Feet apart. T motion.

HOLD TIGHT *(clap)* EAGLES *(clap)* LET'S FIGHT *(clap)*

(pause)
Broken T.

Hold Tight
Place your right arm over your left arm flat in front of your chest.

(pause)
Clap.

Eagles
Low V.

(pause)
Clap.

Let's Fight
High V.

(pause)
Clap.

SHOOT *(pause)* SHOOT *(pause)* TAKE IT TO THE HOOP *(clap)*

Shoot
Feet apart. Arms in touchdown.

(pause)
Daggers.

Shoot
High V.

(pause)

Nod head while continuing high V.

Take It

Grab hands over your head in a circle.

To The

With a firm grasp of your hands, circle arms around and down to the right.

Hoop

Circle arms back up again to the right.

(pause)

Clap. Repeat.

B-E-A-T. BEAT THOSE BEARS

B
Here is another good time to use your pom-poms. Left hip dip. Right arm on hip. Left arm in low V.

E
Right hip dip. Right arm in low V. Left arm on hip.

A
Left hip dip. Right arm on hip. Left arm in low V.

T

Right hip dip. Right arm in low V.
Left arm on hip.

Beat

Stand straight feet apart. Clap.

Those

Stay in position. Clap again.

Bears
High V.

SHOOT *(clap clap clap)* SHOOT *(clap clap clap)* SHOOT *(clap)*

Shoot
Feet apart. Right
arm punch up.
Left arm on hip.

(pause)
Clap.

(pause)
Clap.

FOR *(clap)* TWO *(clap clap clap)*

(pause)
Clap.

Shoot
Right arm punch up. Left arm on hip.

(pause)
Clap.

(pause)
Clap.

(pause)
Clap.

Shoot
High V.

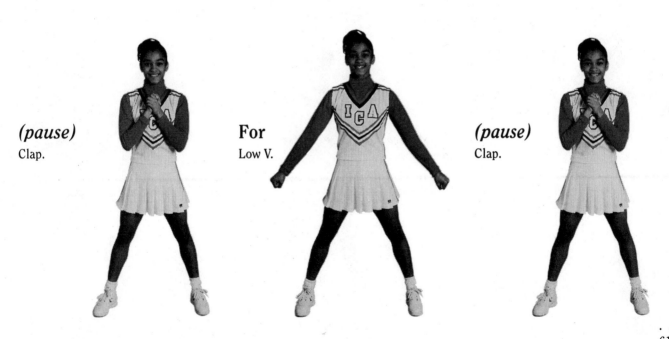

(pause)
Clap.

For
Low V.

(pause)
Clap.

Two
High V.

(pause)
Clap.

(pause)
Clap.

(pause)
Clap.

EAGLES *(clap)* WE'RE TOO HOT, TOO HOT TO STOP

Eagles

Again, let's use
your pom-poms.
Feet apart.
Low V.

(pause)

Clap.

We're Too

Right arm in
dagger. Left arm
on hip.

Hot

Right arm
punch up.
Left arm on
hip.

Too

Bring right arm
back down to
daggers.

Hot

Punch
right arm
up again.

To

Step out to right
lunge. Arms in
low touchdown.

Stop

Stand straight
up, feet apart.
Hands on hips.

Chapter 5 CHEERS

Now you are ready to move on to more challenging things. That's right, it's time to learn some cheers! They are almost exactly like the chants you have been working on, only they are a little bit longer and slower. Don't forget to make those motions sharp. Each motion should pop to the next one like a rubber band that you snap across the room. At the same time, you want to make sure that you are snapping each motion into exactly the right place. Think about each one and exactly where it should be placed. And don't forget to smile! Ready? Here we go!

WE ARE THE BEST *(clap)* BETTER THAN THE REST *(clap)*

Ready
(pause) OK
Stand straight
with feet apart.

We
Low V.

Are The
Clap.

Score *(pause)* Six More *(clap)* Eagles *(pause)* Oh Yes!

Best
High V.

(pause)
Clap.

Better
Broken T.

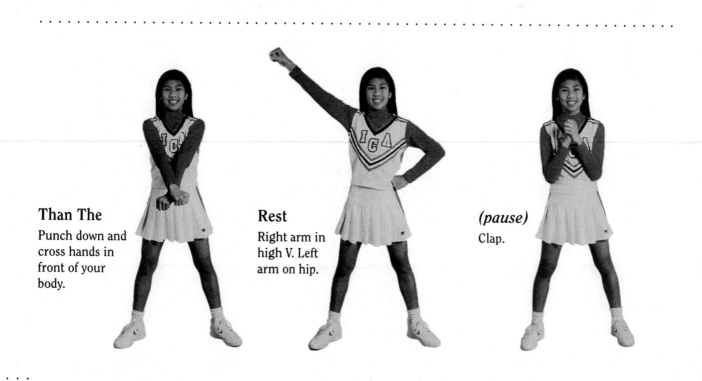

Than The
Punch down and cross hands in front of your body.

Rest
Right arm in high V. Left arm on hip.

(pause)
Clap.

Score
Touchdown
motion.

(pause)
Daggers.

Six More
Touchdown
motion
again.

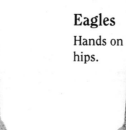

(pause)
Clap.

Eagles
Hands on
hips.

(pause)
Step back
into a front
lunge, right leg
bent, keeping
hands on hips.

Oh Yes!

Stay in lunge
and hit a high V.

EAGLES *(clap)* HOLD TIGHT *(clap)* RED AND WHITE *(clap)*

Ready
(pause)
OK

Stand straight
up, feet apart,
hands on
hips.

Eagles
High V.

(pause)
Clap.

GET THAT BALL *(clap)* FIGHT EAGLES FIGHT!

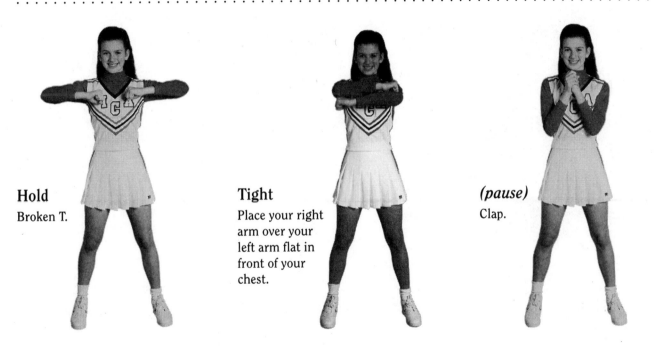

Hold
Broken T.

Tight
Place your right arm over your left arm flat in front of your chest.

(pause)
Clap.

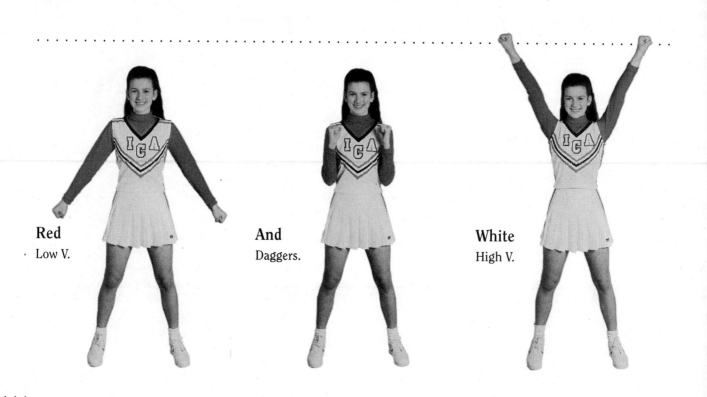

Red
Low V.

And
Daggers.

White
High V.

(pause)
Clap.

Get
Step out to a left lunge (left leg bent). Left arm on hip, right across body.

That
Stand up straight, feet apart. Broken right diagonal.

Ball
Open up to a
right diagonal.

(pause)
Clap.

Fight
Right arm in
low V.
Left arm
on hip.

78

Eagles

Switch it
to the right
arm in
low V.
Left on
hip.

Fight!

High V.

YELL FOR THE EAGLES *(clap)* WE CAN'T BE BEAT *(clap)*

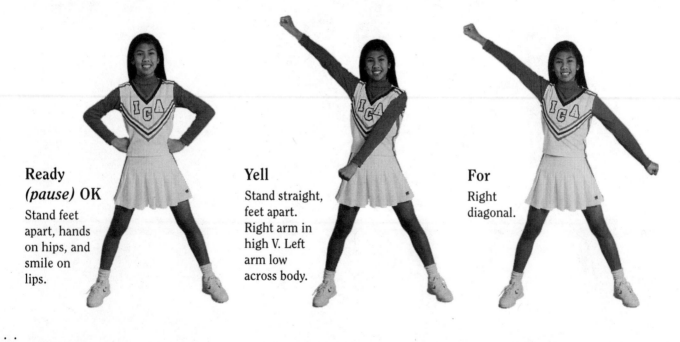

Ready
(pause) OK

Stand feet
apart, hands
on hips, and
smile on
lips.

Yell

Stand straight,
feet apart.
Right arm in
high V. Left
arm low
across body.

For

Right
diagonal.

So Watch Out *(clap)* Panthers *(clap)*

The Eagles
Move left
arm up
to high V.

(pause)
Clap.

We
Daggers.

WE'LL KNOCK YOU OFF YOUR FEET!

Can't Be
Swing arms down, a little past your hips, and back up.

Beat
Continue to swing up to punch out.

(pause)
Clap.

So
Watch Out
Right
diagonal.

(pause)
Clap.

Panthers
Left diagonal.

. . .

83

(pause)
Clap.

We'll Knock

Kneel down
on your right
knee. Right arm
on hip, left
punch up.

You Off

Right arm on
hip, bring left
arm down to
daggers.

Your Feet!

Drop down to
your seat. Left
arm in high V,
right on hips.

FIRE UP TO GO, IT'S TIME TO FIGHT *(pause)*

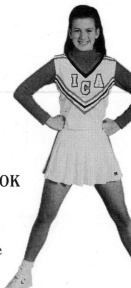  

Ready
(pause) OK
Stand
straight,
hands on
hips, smile
on lips!

Fire
Hop your feet
together, and dip
a little. Arms in
daggers.

Up
Stand up tall,
keeping feet
together. Arms
shoot up to
touchdown.

LET'S GO EAGLES *(clap)* WIN TO-NIGHT!

To Go

Step out with
your right foot
to a left lunge.
Arms in a T.

It's Time
(short pause)

Step over to
your left foot,
lift right to a
liberty hitch.
Left arm across,
to your right
knee. Right arm
on hip.

To Fight
(short pause)

Hop out
feet apart.
Arms
move to
high V.

Let's
Arms move
to daggers.

Go
Left L
motion.

Eagles
Lower
right
arm
to a T.

(pause)
Clap.

Win
Broken T.

To-
Punch broken T down to cross low in front of your body.

Night!

Right arm in
high V. Left
arm on hip.

TIGERS YOU'RE THROUGH *(clap)* WE'RE COMING AFTER YOU

Ready
(pause) OK
Stand feet apart.
Hands on hips.
Smile.

(pause)
Clap.

Tigers
Step your right
leg out to a left
lunge. Arms
in a T
motion.

(clap) YOU'VE MET THE BEST FROM EAST TO WEST

You're

Bring arms straight down and clap.

Through

Stand up straight, feet apart. Right arm punch up, left on hip.

(pause)

Clap.

TIGERS YOU'RE THROUGH!

We're Coming
Daggers.

Af-ter
Punch up to Daggers.

You
Bring right arm to your hip. Left arm comes to front punch.

(pause)
Clap.

You've Met
Keep your
hands clasped
and shoot
them out
in front of
your body.

The Best
Keep your
arms straight
and shoot
out to
high V.

. . .
94

From East

Lower right arm to T, look to the right. Bring left to your hip.

To West

Switch it to right arm on hip. Left arm in T and head turned to left.

Tigers

Clasp. Feet hop together.

You're
Dip low keeping head up, arms straight down at your shins.

Through!
Pop out so that feet are apart. Arms in high V.

STAND UP, IT'S TIME TO SHOUT, COME ON CROWD, YELL IT OUT

Ready
(pause) OK

Stand straight,
feet together
hands on hips,
smile on lips!

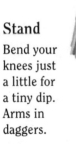

Stand

Bend your
knees just
a little for
a tiny dip.
Arms in
daggers.

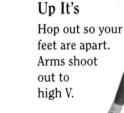

Up It's

Hop out so your
feet are apart.
Arms shoot
out to
high V.

GO FIGHT WIN *(clap)* GO FIGHT WIN, AGAIN, GO FIGHT WIN!

Time
Low V.

To
Bend your
arms to
a broken
low V.

Shout
Bring them
out again to
a low V.

Come

From low V cross arms in front and begin to circle them up.

On

Continue to circle arms up and over your head.

Crowd

Circle them back all the way around to a low V again.

Yell It
Clap.

Out
Clap.

Go
Right arm
punch straight
up. Left arm
on hip.

Fight

Bring right
arm to dagger.
Keeping left
on hip.

Win

Shoot right
arm to a
punch
again.

(pause)

Clap.

Go

Again right
arm punches
up. Left arm
goes to hip.

Fight

Bring right
arm down
to dagger.

Win

Punch right
arm up
again.

Again

Clap.

Go

Punch left
arm up. Right
arm on hip.

Fight

Bring left arm
down to
daggers.
Right stays
on hip.

Win

Shoot right leg
out to a left lunge.
Arms both shoot
out to a high V.

Chapter 6 JUMPS

As a cheerleader, it is your job to keep the crowd excited and fired up, and jumps are the best way to do just that! A great jump is probably the most impressive thing that a cheerleader can do for the fans. But jumps are also the most difficult skill to perfect. You have to have very strong muscles and good flexibility first, then you have to get all the right body parts moving at the same time.

Let's start with jump training, which means doing some exercises that will help get your muscles stronger and prepare them for those super jumps you will soon be showing off. These exercises will help

. . .
105

you get your jumps higher in the air. They will also help you to combine your head, arm, shoulder, and leg movements so that you will have the makings of a perfect jump.

After we've done the jump training, we'll try some real jumps. Try to learn each jump before going on to the next. But before you begin, make sure that you have stretched all your muscles and are really warmed up. Now, let's get started!

WALKING LUNGE

Standing with feet together, raise up your left leg to a liberty hitch, and lift your arms to a touchdown. Keep your body tall, your tummy tucked in, and your head up; lift up on your right toe.

Now step out on your left leg into a great big lunge and move your arms to a T.

Keep moving. Step on to your left leg and lift up your right into a liberty hitch. Shoot your arms back up to a touchdown. Get ready to make a giant lunge again. You should try 10 big lunges.

LEG BOUNDERS

You are just going to leap into the air as high as you can. Use your arms to help you by swinging them at your sides.

As you leap up, bring one leg up to a hitch position. Land on the hitched foot, and jump up again and bring the other foot up.

Then start all over again on the first foot. Do about 10 bounders on each leg, so you will count to 20!

SPEED TUCKS

These are better if they are not done on cement but a softer surface, such as grass or an exercise mat. Start with your feet together and your arms in a high V.

Now jump, keeping your shoulders and head up (this helps you get "hang time" in the air). Bring your knees to your chest. Try to keep your arms in a high V.

As your legs come back to the ground keep your head, chest, and shoulders up high.

Then shoot back up again as fast as you can. You should keep jumping fast without stopping so that you look like a cartoon person going boing! boing! boing!

APPROACHES

Once you have worked hard on your exercises, you are ready to learn how to do a jump. The approach is the first thing to learn because that is what gets your jumps started.

Stand on your toes with your arms in a high V. Make sure that your head, shoulders, and chest are up high.

Bend your knees and swing your arms quickly down in front of your body.

Now jump up with all your might, using your arm swing to help you get your body higher off the ground.

Work on the approach a few times just going straight up in the air before you try to put jumps with it.

Now we're ready to learn some real jumps! Let's go!

JUMPS

Tuck

You jump straight up in the air with your head, shoulders, and chest up, and bring your knees to your chest. Make sure you keep your feet together. Don't forget to point your toes!

Sailor Tuck

This is very much like a tuck because you still need to keep your upper body high, but now you will change your hand positions to look like a sailor. Right arm salutes, left arm on hip!

Spread Eagle

When you do a spread eagle, your arms go into a high V and your legs go straight out to the sides. Your knees and your shoelaces should be facing the crowd. Point your toes again!

Stag

This jump is a little harder. Now you have to remember that your upper body needs to stay nice and tall, with your arms in a high V. This time your legs are going to be in different positions. One will bend up really close to your body and the other will shoot out straight behind your back.

Abstract

This one's even more difficult. Your arms and upper body are the same, but your legs are going to bend in all different directions. One will bend in half in front of your body and the other will bend in half behind your body. It will be easier to get used to this position if you do it sitting on the ground first.

Hurdler

I bet you've noticed that all the jumps get harder. Well, that's because you are getting better. Now for the hurdler. Again, your upper body stays the same, but your legs change. One leg will go straight out in front of you as high as you can get it, and your other leg is going to bend out to the side of your body. Again, you can try this one on the ground to get used to the position.

Toe Touch

This is probably the most popular jump, and the hardest. You have to remember to keep your head, chest, and shoulders nice and high. Your arms are not going to be in a high V but out to your sides, like they are going to touch your toes (though they don't really touch). Now you need to jump up, using your arms and shoulders to get really high off the ground. Swing your legs right up to your body (don't bring your body to your legs as that will make your jump lower). This time your knees and shoelaces will face up to the sky. And don't forget to point your toes!

Jumps are awesome for getting the crowd fired up! You can do them before a cheer, after a cheer, or in the middle of a cheer to make them even more fun for your fans to watch!

Jumps are also great when your team does something super! They take a lot of practice and are not simple to perfect, but with hard work, you will have great jumps. Just have patience and work on your jump training and don't forget to stretch.

Congratulations! You are now ready to go out and cheer! In fact, let's do one of the cheers you have already learned and put a jump in it.

WE ARE THE BEST *(clap)* BETTER THAN THE REST *(clap)*

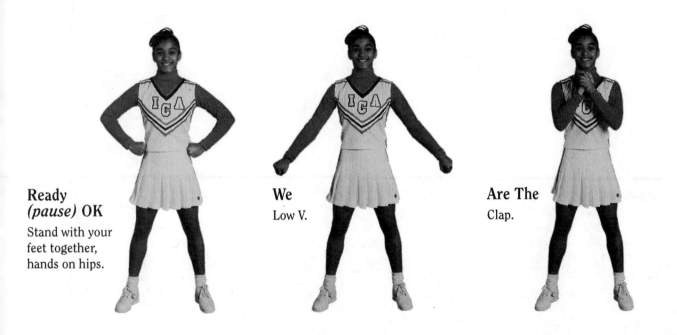

Ready
(pause) OK

Stand with your
feet together,
hands on hips.

We
Low V.

Are The
Clap.

SCORE *(pause pause)* SIX MORE *(clap)* EAGLES OH YES!

Best
High V.

(pause)
Clap.

Better
Broken T.

Than The

Shoot your half
T to punch low
in front of your
body.

Rest

Right arm in
high V. Left arm
on hip.

(pause)

Clap.

Score

High V preparation on your toes (get ready here comes the jump!).

(pause pause)

The two pauses are you doing your jump (shown here as a tuck).

Six More

When you land your jump, pop out so your feet are apart; hit a touchdown.

(pause)
Clap.

Eagles
Step back with your left leg to a right leg front lunge. Hands on hips.

Oh Yes!
Hit a high V!!
Great Job!!!